Golden Tips
for those
Golden Years

Healthy Life Choices that Enhance Longevity

Sharon Platt-McDonald

*Copyright © 2014 Stanborough Press Ltd
Printed 2014.
Reprinted 2014.*

All rights reserved. No part of this publication may be reproduced in any form without prior permission from the publisher.

*British Library Cataloguing in Publication Data.
A catalogue record for this book is available from the British Library.*

ISBN: 978-1-909545-23-6

Published by the Stanborough Press Ltd, Alma Park, Grantham, Lincolnshire, UK.

Illustrated by Abigail Murphy.

Printed in China.

Golden Tips for those Golden Years

Healthy Life Choices that Enhance Longevity

Sharon Platt-McDonald

Golden Tips for those Golden Years

Contents

A word to begin 6
The golden eight 10
Air 12
    The power of air
    Air and breathing exercises
    Air quality impact
    Healthy air tips
Sunshine 20
    Adequate sunshine
    Testimonials
    Sunshine – the healer
Self-control 27
    How controlled are you?
    How balanced are you?
    Mavis's testimonial
    Exercise for you to try
Rest 32
    The value of rest
    Rest – do you get enough?
    Practical tips

Contents

Exercise 39
    Jillian's testimony
    Exercise – the health benefit
    Exercise – what are you doing?
    Age-related exercise

Diet 50
    Are you eating right?
    What's on your plate?
    Food as medicine
    Health foods

Water 61
    Water benefits
    Water – how much is enough?
    Factors influencing water requirements
    Getting the balance right
    Water intoxication
    Dehydration
    Water – therapeutic external use

Trust in God 71
    Faith and healing
    The Adventist impact

Maintaining health during illness 76
    A personal perspective

A final word 79

Golden Tips for those Golden Years

A word to begin

If you knew of eight things that would likely guarantee a long, healthy and happy life, would you put them on your 'must do' list? I would hope so. Well, research at the Weimar Institute has provided just such a list – the 'eight natural doctors' – the keys to longevity. These are: Nutrition; Exercise; Water; Sunlight; Temperance (balance); Air; Rest; and Trust. Also known as NEWSTART,[1] which is the acronym for these eight key factors, they form a prescription of 'natural healers' to assist us on our journey through life. In a moment we will take a brief look at each one of them.

So, what are the latest facts about ageing, and how many of us will make it to a good old age, or even be able to enjoy the golden years? Well, in answer to those questions, Alexander Chancellor in *The Guardian* of Friday 6 August 2010 made this insightful statement:

'The Queen's practice of sending telegrams to people on their 100th birthdays can hardly continue forever when the country is to be flooded with centenarians. Official statistics published yesterday showed life expectancy increasing at such a rate that a quarter of all babies born this year are expected to live to more than 100. Buckingham Palace will not be able to cope, nor will it want to, since reaching 100

Golden Tips for those Golden Years

will have become a very ordinary achievement. Already, there are more than 10,000 centenarians in Britain, compared to only about 100 a century ago.'

It's a fact that the British are living longer as a nation. Average life expectancy in England and Wales is 83 years for women and 79 years for men.[2] However, due to factors such as declining birth and death rates, increased life expectancy as a result of higher living standards, and improved welfare and medical services, the chances of reaching 100 are more favourable than they used to be.

Living a long life is admirable, but living it in relatively good health is even more so. Minimising the effects of ageing is less about science and more about body maintenance. Thomas Edison wrote in several newspapers in 1902:

'The doctor of the future will give no medicine, but will instruct his patient in the care of the human frame, in diet, and in the cause and prevention of disease.'[3]

So what makes us age well? Perhaps it's best to learn from the three places on Earth where people live the longest: Okinawa; Sardinia; and Loma Linda, California. On 19 February 2008, a BBC 2 *Horizon* documentary revealed findings from a 30-year stretch of research by Drs Bradley and Craig Wilcox (brothers), scientists who followed these three communities. Here's what they found:

- In a population of 1 million people, the Okinawans have more than 900 centenarians, a ratio which is more than four times higher than the UK or USA. The Okinawans follow a mainly vegetarian diet and

A word to begin

exercise well into old age. Dr Bradley Wilcox stated: 'If we lived in the West more like the Okinawans, we could probably close 80 per cent of our cardiovascular units and a third of our cancer wards, and nursing homes would go out of business.'

- The Sardinians have a genetic predisposition, which gives them an advantage. The absence of the G6PD enzyme due to a faulty X chromosome gene has been responsible for the longevity of the Ovodda community in Sardinia. However, they also tend to emphasise good social connections and adhere to a largely Mediterranean diet (although it does include meat).
- In Loma Linda, California, the Seventh-day Adventists were found to live 10 years longer than their American counterparts. The positive impact of a vegetarian diet, not smoking, not drinking, a disciplined lifestyle, faith, and stress-reduced living were indicated as key factors in their longevity. During the study, Adventist surgeon, Dr Elsworth Wareham, was filmed undertaking open heart surgery at age 92.

In the following chapters we analyse some of the current research on the 'golden eight' we mentioned earlier and their impact on longevity. In addition, we will highlight some case studies that exemplify the benefits of these natural health principles.

[1] *The NEWSTART acronym was developed by the Weimar Institute (A Health Lifestyle Centre in the US).*
[2] www.ons.gov.uk/ons/dcp171778_332904.pdf
[3] *As listed at:* www.snopes.com/quotes/futuredoctor.asp

Golden Tips for those Golden Years

The golden eight

'Pure air, sunlight, abstemiousness, rest, exercise, proper diet, the use of water, trust in divine power – these are the true remedies. Every person should have a knowledge of nature's remedial agencies and how to apply them.' Ellen G. White, *The Ministry of Healing,* page 127.

The above quotation is often referred to as containing the 'golden eight', as it identifies the eight natural health laws whose well-researched principles have been found to be advantageous to health and well-being. It is these eight health principles that we highlight in this little volume, using current research and case studies to examine their efficacy for longevity.

The golden eight

Golden Tips for those Golden Years

Air

The power of air

In the book *The Ministry of Healing*, in the chapter entitled 'In contact with nature', the author writes: 'Physicians and nurses should encourage their patients to be much in the open air. Outdoor life is the only remedy that many invalids need. It has a wonderful power to heal diseases caused by the excitements and excesses of fashionable life. . . .' This was written over 100 years ago, but how relevant is this advice today? Let's examine the following case study. . . .

Air

Marge's testimonial

An asthmatic for several years, Marge was maintained on daily medication to assist her breathing. When she joined the CHIP programme[1] in 2008 she was introduced to a healthy lifestyle that made a positive impact on her well-being. After adjusting her diet, introducing an exercise routine and getting more rest she saw her symptoms reduce significantly. The major impact, however, was on her respiratory health. She states:

'I began outdoor walks early in the morning and found that my breathing was easier throughout the day. However, when I commenced deep-breathing exercises (usually outdoors when the air was fresh or standing by an open window) several times a day, the change was dramatic. When I went back to the asthma clinic my peak flow readings (measuring lung capacity) had improved. I also found that I was using my reliever inhaler much less as my asthmatic attacks had reduced. I can certainly say that good-quality air and breathing exercises helped me tremendously.'

Facts

- When we take in air through our lungs our red blood cells pick up the oxygen they carry and transport it to the cells in our body.
- Our cells then use this continuous supply of oxygen to produce energy through a process called metabolism.

Golden Tips for those Golden Years

- It is clear, therefore, that an adequate supply of oxygen is necessary to sustain the health of all our cells and the well-being of our bodies.
- By contrast, when we constantly breathe in stale air, we deprive our cells of what they need to enhance well-being and for our bodies to function optimally.

Air and breathing exercises

Today, numerous scientific studies demonstrate the health benefits of fresh air and the adverse effects of polluted air.

Researchers from the Department of General Practice and Primary Care at the University of Aberdeen performed a randomised controlled trial (research designed to examine whether one method is more effective than another) to determine whether formal breathing training improves quality of life and control of asthma. One group received breathing training from respiratory therapists, while the other group received standard asthma education from nurses.

Results from the six-month follow-up indicated a significant improvement in quality-of-life scores in the group who received training-in-breathing exercises, compared to the group who just followed traditional asthma education. Additionally, the levels of anxiety and depression had also decreased among the group who had received respiratory training.

This study, published in the journal *Thorax* (2008), concluded that, while the research did not demonstrate a

Air

decreased need for asthma medication, breathing training could benefit patients whose asthma impairs their quality of life.

So why is correct breathing so important? Deep breathing expands the diaphragm, encouraging more air into the lungs and improving the uptake of oxygen to our cells. The most beneficial locations for deep breathing are natural environments and open spaces where the air is less polluted.

Individuals with asthma, lung disorders and heart disease are more at risk of adverse reactions from poor air quality. They can experience a range of symptoms, including respiratory discomfort, breathing difficulties and chest tightness.

The World Health Organisation (WHO) Air Quality and Health Factsheet No. 313 (September 2011) highlighted the following facts:

- Air pollution is a major environmental risk to health. By reducing air pollution levels, we can help countries reduce the global burden of disease from respiratory infections, heart disease, and lung cancer.
- The lower the levels of air pollution in a city, the better the respiratory (both long- and short-term) and cardiovascular health of the population will be.
- Indoor air pollution is estimated to cause approximately 2 million premature deaths, mostly in developing countries.
- Urban outdoor air pollution is estimated to cause 1.3 million deaths worldwide per year.

Golden Tips for those Golden Years

- The WHO air quality guidelines set criteria for cutting air-quality-related deaths. (An online copy of the guidelines is available from *www.who.int/mediacentre/factsheets/fs313/en*)

Air quality impact

On 3 October 2011 ITV broadcast a documentary titled *Exposure: The Factory*, featuring the ArcelorMittal steel plant in Ostrava, Czech Republic. Regarded as the most polluted city in Europe, Ostrava's poor air quality has been blamed on the emissions from this steel plant. Subsequently, in January 2010, a smog alert was issued when poisonous particles in the air reached concentration levels of 700 or 800 micrograms per cubic metre per hour, in excess of the norm of 50.

Commenting on the findings in a radio interview with Jan Velinger on Radio Praha (29 January 2010), Dr Josef Keder, a specialist at the Hydrometeorological Institute, states: 'It is of course very dangerous for people's health, because particles can penetrate into the respiratory tract, into the lungs, and irritate the tract. . . . Sometimes carcinogenic items or micro-organisms which can cause this

Air

disease can bind to the particles. That is the threat.'

Air pollution can adversely impact health, depending on the type of pollutant, its concentration, the length of time for which our lungs have been exposed to it and our general state of health. If you are concerned about excess exposure to pollutants and are experiencing poor health, you can consult your physician for advice and request to be tested for blood toxins.

Golden Tips for those Golden Years

Seeking ways to ensure that we are exposed to good air is a key factor in maintaining well-being. Try implementing the following:

Healthy air tips

- Open windows regularly, particularly in the early morning and late evening when the air is likely to be cleaner. Keeping doors open also helps increase the transfer of air.
- During your work breaks take deep, slow breaths in outdoor air, away from traffic pollution.
- Undertake deep-breathing exercises daily.
- Exercise daily, preferably outdoors.
- Maintain good posture – sitting upright and standing tall enables lung expansion, which encourages better oxygen intake.
- Make your home a smoke-free zone, and avoid second-hand tobacco smoke wherever possible.
- Avoid breathing in car exhaust fumes, and don't let your car idle near your house windows or in the garage.
- Avoid being in stuffy rooms for lengthy periods.
- Maintain heating and air-conditioning units regularly.
- Ensure cookers, dryers, fireplaces and heaters are properly vented to the outdoors.
- Ensure air ducts and fireplaces are regularly cleaned.
- Have plants in both your home and work environments to help improve air quality, as plants produce oxygen and absorb carbon dioxide from the air.

Air

- Avoid using artificial air fresheners and fragrances in your home. Natural alternatives like citrus, essential oils and spices in a pot with water are far healthier.

[1] *Complete Health Improvement Programme (CHIP) –
See more at* www.sdachip.org

Golden Tips for those Golden Years

Sunshine

The BBC Two *Horizon* documentary aired on 19 February 2008 highlighted the benefits of sunshine and its impact on the centenarians interviewed during the programme. The researchers found that the Okinawans, Sardinians and Loma Linda residents they interviewed spent significant amounts of time outdoors. The report noted that their temperate climates encouraged outdoor activities and much good exposure to the sun. This kept the seniors agile well into their nineties and beyond.

Sunshine

Research indicates that our bodies need natural sunlight to synthesise adequate amounts of vitamin D, which is required for healthy strong bones as well as immune system support.

Scientists at Idaho State University have suggested that poor exposure to sunshine can lead to vitamin D deficiency, which may increase the risk of prostate cancer. In an interview with Richard Alleyne, science correspondent, Dr Sophie St-Hilaire, lead scientist on the study, states: 'We found that colder weather, and low rainfall, were strongly correlated with prostate cancer.' (*The Telegraph*, 21 April 2010.) Other research indicates that poor morbidity and increased mortality are also associated with inadequate exposure to sunlight (*Circulation* – 'The "Sunshine Deficit" and Cardiovascular Disease', Wallis et al – *http://circ.ahajournals.org/content/118/14/1476.full*).

Golden Tips for those Golden Years

Adequate sunshine

The real issue is about how much sunlight is required to enhance our health, and how much puts our health at risk? These questions have been hotly debated for years.

The British Association of Dermatologists and National Osteoporosis Society's joint guidance on daily sun exposure recommends that we should get around 10 minutes a day if we are light-skinned, and 20 minutes if we are dark-skinned.

In a BBC Health News report published in December 2010, health correspondent Jane Dreaper wrote: 'New guidance on vitamin D recommends midday sunshine.' She went on to report that: 'Cancer Research UK and the National Osteoporosis Society are among the bodies which agree that "little and frequent" spells in summer sunshine several times a week can benefit your health. The experts now say it is fine to go outside in strong sun in the middle of the day, as long as you cover up or apply sunscreen before your skin goes red.'

In the same report, however, she highlighted the views of other medical professionals who feel that overprotection gives rise to a deficiency in vitamin D levels.

Professor Rona Mackie from the British Association of Dermatologists was quoted as saying: 'Total sun protection with high-factor sun

Sunshine

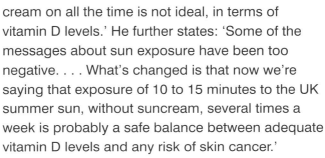

cream on all the time is not ideal, in terms of vitamin D levels.' He further states: 'Some of the messages about sun exposure have been too negative. . . . What's changed is that now we're saying that exposure of 10 to 15 minutes to the UK summer sun, without suncream, several times a week is probably a safe balance between adequate vitamin D levels and any risk of skin cancer.'

The article then went on to state that 'winter levels of vitamin D can be helped by a break in the tropical sun'. Individuals with chronic conditions have found this advice beneficial.

Testimonials

I have spoken to many individuals from Africa, Asia and the Caribbean who take annual trips back to their homeland, not for leisure but for health, because most of them have been diagnosed with low vitamin D levels.

Kofi, whose eczema is classified as being 'severe', found that when he returns to Africa for a holiday each year, his skin 'improves tremendously'.

Isola suffers from arthritis, which gets worse in the winter in spite of the medication she is on. However, she found that since she has commenced annual trips to Barbados (from November to February) she does not experience any symptoms during that period.

Golden Tips for those Golden Years

Sunshine – the healer

Over 150 years ago Ellen G. White highlighted the health and environmental benefits of sunshine. She wrote that: 'Whoever sleeps in a sunless room, or occupies a bed that has not been thoroughly dried and aired, does so at the risk of health . . .' ('General Hygiene', *Ministry of Healing*).

She further asserts that: 'Perfect cleanliness, plenty of sunlight, careful attention to sanitation in every detail of the home life, are essential to freedom from disease and to the cheerfulness and vigour of the inmates of the home.' (*Ministry of Healing*, p. 276.)

Today scientists continue to report the health benefits of safe levels of sun exposure. The Vitamin D Council now suggests that due to previous health reports on the dangers of sun overexposure, people have become frightened of getting skin cancers and so avoided sunshine, to the detriment of their health. (*Vitamin D News*, 18 October 2011.)

In a joint study between Norway's Institute for Cancer Research in Oslo and the US Department of Energy's Brookhaven National Laboratory, it was reported that the health benefits from some sun exposure are far greater than any risk from skin cancer (*The Telegraph*, 7 January 2008 – 'Sunshine – vitamin D and heart disease protection included', Roger Highfield, science editor). Study researcher Johan Moan reported that although certain foods contain vitamin D, the body's main source is from modest sun exposure, which yields greater vitamin D levels.

Dr Michael Holick, author of the book *The UV Advantage*,

Sunshine

is recognised worldwide as a leading authority on vitamin D and the health benefits of natural sunlight, and more than thirty years of his research is detailed at *www.UVadvantage.org*. He states: 'We started realising that people who live in higher latitudes are more prone to vitamin D deficiency and are more prone to developing common cancers and dying of them, such as cancer of the

Golden Tips for those Golden Years

colon, prostate, breast and even ovaries. And we think that that's in part due to the body's inability to make enough activated vitamin D to help regulate cell growth and to keep cell growth in check.

Sunlight has also been found to be beneficial for our emotional health and well-being. Sun exposure helps regulate two mood-controlling hormones, melatonin and serotonin, which boost mental well-being and can be low in those suffering from depression and seasonal affective disorder. Serotonin levels can dip in winter with reduced sunlight. Biological psychologist Lance Workman's research at Bath Spa University suggests that over 90 per cent of people experience a lift in mood with periods of increased sunlight (MSN Him, 20 July 2011). So make sure you get your daily dose whenever possible.

Self-control

A great deal of research points to the wisdom of having balance in our lives. By this we mean that equilibrium where equal attention is given to physical, emotional, social and spiritual health needs without overdoing one or the other.

The importance of social and emotional health was examined by research author Julianne Holt-Lunstad, PhD, associate psychology professor at Brigham Young University in Provo, Utah. The study, published in July 2010, found that, in terms of long life, maintaining strong social ties can be as important as good physiological health practices.

But is there sufficient current scientific evidence that self-control can be health-enhancing?

How controlled are you?

A WebMD Health News report on 24 January 2011 carried the headline 'Self-control in childhood brings adult success'. In it, author Brenda Goodman reviewed a 32-year research study published in *Proceedings of the National Academy of Sciences*, which followed a group of almost 1,000 New Zealanders from birth. It was found that those with lower scores in self-control were significantly more likely to suffer chronic health problems like gum disease and high blood pressure and be overweight than those with

Golden Tips for those Golden Years

high self-control. As adults, the low scorers were more likely to have difficulty managing finances, relationship breakdowns and addiction to alcohol and drugs. They were also more likely to have a criminal record.

Seven per cent of participants demonstrated a significant improvement to their self-control, which was possibly attributable to factors such as the schools they attended, where structure and achievement were stressed, or significant positive changes they had experienced in family life.

Impulse control has become a scientific study as research has revealed differences between the brains of individuals who exercise self-control and those who find it difficult. It appears that making dietary decisions – for example, to avoid a tempting high-calorie dish in favour of something healthier – is easier for some than others, according to a report from *ScienceDaily* (30 April 2009). The report, 'Mechanisms of

Self-control

Self-Control Pinpointed In Brain', reveals that we all use the same area of the brain to make value-based decisions, and another area which modulates activity based on our decisions. It is this area that is more active in people with higher self-control.

In a separate report, Colin Camerer, the Robert Kirby Professor of Behavioural Economics, states: 'After centuries of debate in social sciences we are finally making big strides in understanding self-control from watching the brain resist temptation directly.' (Social Neuroeconomics – ScienceDirect. *Trends in Cognitive Sciences*, volume 11, issue 10, October 2007.)

The next time you visit eating places where the caption 'Eat as much as you like' beckons the appetite to indulge to its full capacity and the urge for self-restraint and moderation is stifled – think again!

How balanced are you?

In most lifestyle programmes today you will most likely hear the words 'balance', 'self-control' or 'temperance' used to denote a lifestyle void of excesses, where emotional, physical, spiritual and social needs are equally met.

In the well-being seminars that I run I

Golden Tips for those Golden Years

have devised a tool called *Transformation Worksheet*, which gives participants an opportunity to assess the level of balance in their lives currently and whether there are any obvious areas of concern. Here's one evaluation from someone attending one of the seminars. . . .

Mavis's testimonial

'I had not realised how out of balance my life was until I undertook the exercise. I had so much on my plate and so many tasks to accomplish in a 24-hour period that I was sacrificing sufficient rest and adequate sleep to get things done. Then when I became ill with a stress-related disorder, I became impatient with God for healing. When my health deteriorated, it affected my spiritual life too, affecting my capacity to pray, read the Bible and spend adequate time on my devotions. Six weeks after implementing the action points in the *Transformation Worksheet* I saw a significant improvement in my health. I had rearranged my daily schedule to include times for reflection, rest and exercise and as a result was able to spend time on nurturing my spiritual life. I see now how excess in one area can adversely impact another, and I don't want to go there again!'

Do you feel that you currently pay sufficient attention to your emotional, physical, spiritual and social needs without being excessive in any area, or are you looking for more balance in your life? Here is a quick exercise to try. . . .

Divide a blank sheet of paper into four sections, with the

Self-control

headings: Emotional, Physical, Spiritual, Social. In each of the segments write down all the activities you do that relate to that heading. Think about the value you place on each activity; the time allocated to it; and what outcomes you have observed from the frequency, duration and intensity of that activity. This gives you an idea of where you are placing more emphasis in your life. It will also help you ascertain whether you need to pursue a more balanced lifestyle or not.

Golden Tips for those Golden Years

Rest

A 2005 study by Kumar found that disruption of our circadian rhythm (body clock) because of inadequate sleep and rest had physiological repercussions: including reduced lifespan. (*Chronobiology International*, 2005, vol. 22, no. 4.)

Research from the National Sleep Foundation suggests that workaholics are more likely to be depressed, anxious and angry, and have more health complaints and shorter lifespans, than their non-workaholic counterparts. It appears that the chronic stress of constant work can lead to significant physical and mental health problems, which may affect our lifespan. Adequate sleep is essential to recharge your body and assist in maintaining your general well-being.

Study recommendations from the foundation state that adults need 7 to 9 hours of sleep each night. Lead study researcher Lela R. McKnight-Eily, PhD, told *U.S. Medicine* that while it may not be 'uncommon' to have a few bad nights of rest in a given month, the cumulative impact of this can be detrimental. She goes on to state: 'Chronic sleep loss and sleeping disorders themselves are associated with any number of physical and mental health problems, including obesity, hypertension, diabetes, depression, anxiety, and high cholesterol and mortality.'

Golden Tips for those Golden Years

(Institute of Medicine, *Sleep Disorders and Sleep Deprivation: An Unmet Public Health Problem*, National Academies Press, 2006.)

The value of rest

As I was catching up on some reading over the holiday season I came across a magazine called *Experience Life*, and the title of one of its articles caught my attention. It was entitled 'The Dangers of Doing Too Much' and the author, Pilar Gerasimo, commenced with the following: 'Hello. My name is Pilar, and I am a chronic over-doer. I'm in recovery now. . . .' She then went on to detail how overwork and lack of adequate rest took its toll on her physical, mental and social life and subsequently led her to make the drastic changes necessary to 'save' her life.

Over 100 years ago Ellen G. White highlighted the dangers of overwork and inadequate rest. Under the heading 'Caution Concerning Overwork' (*Mind, Character and Personality*, volume 2 – 'Harmonious Action of the Whole Personality Necessary') she stated: 'Remember that man must preserve his God-given talent of intelligence by keeping the physical machinery in harmonious action. . . . It is not work but *overwork*, without periods of rest, that breaks people down, endangering the life-forces. Those who overwork soon reach the place where they work in a hopeless way' (emphasis supplied).

In more recent times science has documented its own findings on the importance of rest and the consequences that can ensue when sufficient rest is not attained. An

Rest

online *Daily Mail* health report by Sophie Borland on 5 April 2011 carried this headline: 'Working an 11-hour day can increase heart attack danger by 67 per cent'. The article reported on a study conducted by University College London, which found that individuals with a working day of over 11 hours increased their risk of a heart attack by two thirds. The research team analysed the average daily working hours of more than 7,000 civil servants at Whitehall over an 11-year period. Their medical records and health checks were also looked at to gather information on their heart health. The study, published in the journal *Annals of Internal Medicine*, found that 192 of the subjects had suffered a heart attack. It found that those working over 11 hours a day had a 67 per cent higher risk than those who had jobs with a nine-to-five schedule.

According to the lead researcher, Professor Mika Kivimäki: *'We have shown that working long days is associated with a remarkable increase in risk of heart disease.'* The report suggested that patients already at high risk – for example, those overweight or smokers – could be encouraged to cut down their working hours.

Rest – do you get enough?

Following an injury, I recently experienced some 'enforced rest' and found that making the transition from a generally overflowing weekly agenda to one of relative 'stillness' was indeed challenging. However, looking at the situation from a positive standpoint, I realised that I was getting a lot of practice in living the balanced lifestyle

Golden Tips for those Golden Years

(which included adequate rest) that I teach others to aspire to!

Rest is so important to well-being that Jesus gave a directive to His disciples to pause from the busyness of life to be rejuvenated: 'And He said to them, "Come aside by yourselves to a deserted place and rest a while." For there were many coming and going, and they did not even have time to eat.' Mark 6:31 (NKJV).

Getting the balance right between work and rest is more of a challenge than people think. Whenever I run a session on 'Preventing Burnout', there are always people in attendance who state that they are often too busy in the

Rest

working day to even take a lunch break. On that list of over-busy participants are people in the 'caring' professions who often take their work home with them or find it hard to 'switch off' outside of work. Among them are those in various ministries and those in pressurised environments working to daily deadlines.

Under the heading, 'Work-life balance biggest health concern', the British Psychological Society published an online article (6 January 2012) that indicated work-life balance as the top concern for some employers. It reported on a survey by Group Risk Development (GRiD), which found employees stressed by their working hours, workload

Golden Tips for those Golden Years

and expectations of delivery that interfered with their ability to balance work deadlines and the demands of home life. This impacted negatively on their health and work attendance.

While attending health retreats and presenting on the topic of well-being I have tried many useful 'rest tips'. In addition to a good night's sleep (around 8 hours) try the following:

Practical tips:

- Plan your working day ahead to include a break.
- When working at your desk or computer, take a short break each hour – stand up and stretch or walk around the office.
- Get outside daily in the open air for some deep-breathing exercises to rejuvenate mind and body.
- Have a 'prayer break'. Punctuating my day with brief moments of prayer is restorative.
- Take a power nap (preferably during your break).
- Plan weekend breaks away.
- Holistic activities like regular exercise, massage, country walks, relaxing music and managing stress will enhance your rest.

Exercise

Exercise

A US study from Stanford University led by James Fries, MD, advocated jogging as a key health activity that promotes longevity. The researchers studied 500 runners over the age of 50 and tracked their progress over a twenty-year period. Nineteen years into the study, diverse outcomes from the two groups began to emerge. It was found that 34% of the non-runners had died, compared to only 15% of the runners. (Stanford School of Medicine, 11 August 2008, Erin Digitale.)

Identified as a natural remedy, exercise can make a remarkable difference to our well-being. Jillian shares her experience of outdoor exercise and its rewards:

Jillian's testimony

'Following a GP visit for a medical check I was told that I was morbidly obese. My weight was 317lbs, or 144kg. I was alarmed. I didn't realise I was so huge. I decided to put my life in order and adopt a healthy lifestyle, which I began in August 2011. I commenced applying the CHIP programme, renowned for its positive spiritual, physical and social health outcomes. My exercise programme began immediately. After a failed gym attempt, I began walking for ten minutes a day before going to work until I progressed to

Golden Tips for those Golden Years

45 minutes daily. I loved being in the fresh air and appreciating the beauty of nature. The best part of all was being alone with God. It was on these occasions that most of my prayers were answered, including the strength to commit to a healthy lifestyle. Eventually, the weight began falling off. Within six months I lost 1st 2lbs. To date I am 240lbs, or 109kg. I thank God for this progress daily. Not only do I feel better, but friends and family comment on how much better I look. My greatest blessing, however, is the joy of praising God with a healthy mind, soul, spirit and body.'

Documenting the health benefits of exercise, The US Centres for Disease Control and Prevention identified the following as key positive outcomes:
- Weight control
- Reduced risk of cardiovascular disease
- Reduced risk of type 2 diabetes and metabolic syndrome
- Reduced risk of some cancers
- Strengthening of bones and muscles
- Improved mental health and mood
- Improved vitality and ability to undertake daily activities
- Prevention of falls, particularly in older adults
- Enhancement of longevity.

Visit the following website for more information:
www.cdc.gov/physicalactivity/everyone/health/index.html

Exercise – the health benefits

Exercise

Golden Tips for those Golden Years

In the previous segment we introduced the many health benefits of exercise identified by the US Centres for Disease Control and Prevention. We look at these claims now in more detail.

Weight control
- Weight gain occurs when the calories you burn (including when you exercise) are fewer than the calories generated from your food and drink.
- The physical activity sufficient to burn enough calories to control weight varies from person to person.
- Reducing calorie intake and increasing physical activity generally results in weight loss.

Reduced risk of cardiovascular disease
- Regular physical activity can lower blood pressure and improve cholesterol levels.
- Around 150 minutes a week (2½ hours) of moderate-intensity aerobic activity can lower the risk of cardiovascular disease.

Reduced risk of type 2 diabetes and metabolic

Exercise

syndrome
- A combination of high blood pressure, excess fat around the waist, high blood sugar, and high cholesterol results in a condition called metabolic syndrome.
- With 2½ hours of moderate-intensity aerobic activity each week the risk of type 2 diabetes and metabolic syndrome is reduced.

Reduced risk of some cancers
- Colon cancer risk is lower in physically active people than those who are inactive.
- Breast cancer risk is lower in women who are active than those who are not.
- Endometrial and lung cancer risk is lower with people who exercise regularly compared to those who are inactive.

Strengthening of bones and muscles

Golden Tips for those Golden Years

- Undertaking moderately intense aerobic muscle- and bone-strengthening physical activity can slow the loss of bone density expected with ageing.
- Weekly physical activity over 2 hours lowers the risk of hip fracture and improves arthritis.

Improved mental health and mood

- Regular exercise aids learning, thinking and judgement.
- The risk of depression is reduced and sleep is enhanced through exercising 3-4 times per week.

Improved vitality and ability to undertake daily activities

- Physically active middle-aged and older adults have a lower risk of limited function than inactive people.
- It enhances the ability to climb stairs and engage in other energetic activities.

Prevention of falls, particularly in older adults

- Weekly balance and muscle-strengthening exercises and brisk walks reduce the risk of falls.

Enhancement of longevity

- Physical activity of around 7 hours per week reduces the risk of early death by 40% compared to those active for less than 30 minutes a week.

Exercise

For more information on these health benefits, visit the following website:
www.cdc.gov/physicalactivity/everyone/health

Exercise – what are you doing?

Let's begin with some questions: what types of physical activity do you enjoy? Do you follow a regime? Can you improve on your current exercise routine – or lack of it?

After browsing through health journals and websites, I made a list of at least forty-eight different exercises that you can engage in. The list ranged from aerobics to brisk walks, dance routines to low- and high-impact sports, and gym workouts using Wii-based software. There were exercises you could do at home; at your work desk; indoors, while sitting, standing or lying down; outdoors; in water . . . the list was extensive. None of them included the couch. The message was clear: do something to get moving – and enjoy it!

The 11 July 2011 NHS Choices Information included a report highlighting the new exercise guidelines issued by the Chief Medical Officer. The report established that: 'Adults should do at least 150 minutes of moderate-intensity exercise each week.' This is the minimum required to maintain good health. Also identified was that an optimum fitness programme should include cardiovascular exercise to maintain heart health, stretching exercises for flexibility and resistance exercises for muscle strength and endurance.

When embarking on or evaluating any exercise programme, three key elements to bear in mind are

Golden Tips for those Golden Years

frequency, intensity and duration. NHS recommendations on exercise received from the Department of Health (*www.dh.gov.uk*) give the following guidance:

Frequency – For optimum fitness we should be exercising six times per week.

Intensity – The appropriate intensity varies in individuals and is dependent on age and medical condition. The exercise should be sufficient to raise your heartbeat and make you perspire. Your exercise regime should commence slowly and build up over a period of time.

Duration – Between 45 and 90 minutes of exercise daily is most beneficial for health. However, if you undertake 30 minutes six times per week, positive health outcomes can still be experienced. Some people find that breaking the exercise time into 10-minute segments (morning, afternoon, evening) is more manageable, particularly in the early stages of an exercise programme.

The UK Physical Activity Guidelines published by the Department of Health (11 July 2011) presented evidence that demonstrated the link between physical activity and chronic disease. It was found that sedentary behaviour is an independent risk factor for ill health. So, give the couch a break!

Age-related exercise

We conclude this segment on exercise with a closer look at those guidelines and the survey on exercise published by the Department of Health, 11 July 2011 (*www.dh.gov.uk*).

Exercise

The survey found that only a minority of people in the UK get adequate exercise. Of the recommended 30 minutes' activity on at least five days per week the following percentage of people met the requirements:

- England: 40% of men and 28% of women
- Northern Ireland: 33% of men and 28% of women
- Wales: 36% of men and 23% of women
- Scotland: 43% of men and 32% of women.

Children meeting the required targets:
- England: 32% of boys aged 2-15 and 24% of girls
- Northern Ireland: 19% of boys aged 12-16 and 10% of girls
- Wales: 63% of boys aged 4-15 and 45% of girls
- Scotland: 76% of boys aged 2-15 and 67% of girls.

Golden Tips for those Golden Years

With regard to self-reporting on sedentary behaviour, the survey found that two thirds of adults spend more than 2 hours daily watching TV and using the computer, and spend between 3 and 4 hours seated during their leisure time.

So here is what each age group should be doing to maintain a basic level of health:

Ages 5-18

A minimum of 60 minutes' physical activity daily. This should be a mixture of moderate-intensity activity, like brisk walking, and vigorous-intensity aerobic activity, such as running.

Ages 19-64

A minimum of 150 minutes (2 hours and 30 minutes) of moderate-intensity aerobic activity weekly, such as cycling or brisk walking, is recommended. Additionally, muscle-strengthening activities on 2 or more days weekly that work all major muscle groups such as the chest, shoulders, arms, abdomen, hips, back, and legs.

Alternatively, this age group could engage in 75 minutes (1 hour and 15 minutes) of vigorous-intensity aerobic activity, such as running or a game of singles tennis, weekly.

Ages 65 and above

Older adults aged 65 and above who are in good health with no health conditions limiting their mobility and who are

Exercise

generally fit are encouraged to be active daily.

The recommendations are that they engage in a minimum of 150 minutes (2 hours and 30 minutes) of moderate-intensity aerobic activity, such as cycling or brisk walking, every week. Also included should be muscle-strengthening activities on 2 or more days a week that work the major muscle groups of the chest, shoulders, arms, abdomen, hips, back and legs.

Golden Tips for those Golden Years

Diet

In a BBC *Horizon* documentary aired on 19 February 2008, the Adventist dietary practices were clearly emphasised. The reporter stated that: 'Many Adventists stick to the vegetarian diet encouraged by the Church.' This was shown to be more advantageous in enhancing longevity. Marge Jetton, a Seventh-day Adventist (aged 103 at the time of the interview), attested to the fruits, vegetables, nuts and grains which kept her healthy.

The BBC *Horizon* documentary also examined the dietary habits of the Okinawans, who eat approximately 1,200 calories a day. They live by the belief in a significant cultural

Diet

tradition called 'hara hachi bu', which, translated, means: 'Eat until you're only 80% full, then push away from the table.' This is a stark contrast to cultural habits that drive food consumption in the West. We seem to focus on getting more for our money when we visit food outlets with 'eat as much as you like' offers. We may get our money's worth, but do we get our 'health's worth' by overeating to the point of feeling bloated, then putting our organs under pressure to deal with the excess? Research indicates that a smaller dietary intake may be linked to longevity.

Reporting on 'The China Study', author Dr Colin Campbell found: 'People who ate the most animal-based foods got the most chronic disease . . . people who ate the most plant-based foods were the healthiest and tended to avoid chronic disease and lived longer.' (*The China Study*, 2004, Campbell & Campbell, p. 7.)

Golden Tips for those Golden Years

Are you eating right?

Agreeing on what constitutes *'proper diet'* has been the subject of ongoing debate among various medical professionals and health enthusiasts.

With easy access to the internet, we currently have at our fingertips unlimited information from diverse sources: some medically approved and well researched; others not. Yet all claim to have the answer about what we should eat and why, and how it will benefit us. How do you know which information to trust? What is a *proper diet* anyway?

We often hear of media reports and research indicating that 'eating right' will result in good health outcomes. One such report, featured in an article by Dr Franchesca Harper published by *Livestrong.com* (14 October 2010), states:

'Good eating habits may help people look younger longer, reduce risks for disease and even keep the brain healthy.'

A report in the 12 March 2012 edition of *ProperDiet.com*, 'Diet and Nutrition Simplified', supports this:

'People today are becoming increasingly aware that a *proper diet* is the foundation of good health. If we don't have a regular diet of wholesome food and the essential trace minerals which it provides, we don't have the fuel or the formula to perform at our best' (*www.properdiet.com*).

How does E. G. White's book *Counsels on Diet and Foods*, written over 150 years ago, match up to this current research?

Diet

Your personal evaluation:
Here are some well-researched resources for you to investigate that will help you decide whether or not you are eating right.
- The CHIP programme, with its emphasis on the benefits of a plant-based diet (*http://www.chipuk.org.uk/chipvideo*)
- Dr Clemency Mitchell's latest book, *Understanding Nutrition*, available from the Stanborough Press and most ABC bookstores
- The Adventist Discovery Centre health course entitled: *Your World of Good Food* (*www.discoveronline.org.uk*).

What's on your plate?
Over 100 years ago E. G. White gave some useful advice regarding dietary intelligence.

'*Grains, fruits, nuts, and vegetables constitute the diet chosen for us by our Creator. These foods, prepared in as simple and natural a manner as possible, are the most healthful and nourishing. They impart a strength, a power of endurance, and a vigour of intellect that are not afforded by a more complex and stimulating diet.*' The Ministry of Healing, p. 296.

Today, one medical journal, *The Lancet*, has come to a similar conclusion:

'*Eating a diet rich in plant foods, in the form of fruits, vegetables, and whole-grain cereals, probably remains the best option for reducing the risk of colon cancer, and for more general health protection.*' The Lancet, 361 (3 May, 2003): 1448.

Golden Tips for those Golden Years

So, what's on your plate? *The Full Plate Diet*, although not purely about a plant-based diet, contains excellent information about the portions we should be eating from each food group. It contains advice on how to eat more fruit, vegetables, grains, seeds and nuts, while cutting back on animal products in the move to a more plant-based diet. It focuses on increasing fibre in the diet (*www.FullPlateLiving.org*).

The Full Plate Diet's top five fibre-rich foods in each food group are:

Top five fruits:
1. Raspberries/blackberries – 1 cup (8g fibre),
2. Pears – 1 medium (6g fibre),
3. Apples – 1 medium (4g fibre),
4. Oranges – 1 medium (3g fibre),
5. Bananas – 1 medium (3g fibre).

Top five vegetables:
1. Avocados – 1 medium (14g fibre),
2. Broccoli – 1 cup (5g fibre),
3. Spinach – 1 cup (4g fibre),
4. Carrots – 1 cup (4g fibre),
5. Sweet potatoes – 1 medium (2g fibre).

Top five beans:
1. Navy beans – ½ cup (10g fibre),
2. Lentils – ½ cup (8g fibre),
3. Pinto beans – ½ cup (8g fibre),

Diet

    4. Black beans – ½ cup (8g fibre),
    5. Kidney beans – ½ cup (6g fibre).

Top five nuts & seeds:
    1. Flaxseeds – 1oz (8g fibre),
    2. Almonds – 1oz (4g fibre),
    3. Sunflower seeds – 1oz (2g fibre),
    4. Peanuts – 1oz (2g fibre),
    5. Walnuts – 1oz (2g fibre).

Top five grains:
    1. Wheat – 1 cup (8g fibre),
    2. Pearl barley – 1 cup (6g fibre),
    3. Quinoa – 1 cup (5g fibre),
    4. Oats – 1 cup (4g fibre),
    5. Brown rice – 1 cup (4g fibre).

Eat up!

Golden Tips for those Golden Years

Food as medicine?

One of the best-known quotations on the therapeutic value of food is the following:

'Let food be thy medicine and medicine be thy food.' (Hippocrates, father of medicine, 431 BC.)

Following up on the concept of food as medicine, I spoke recently with Angelette Muller, a nutrition consultant working in an integrated medical clinic, to get her perspective. Here is what she said:

'If you asked me if food was medicine, I would ask what are the similarities between the two? We know that medicine includes treatment and prevention. And diet-related research shows that food can be used both in managing conditions, as well as in reducing the risk for certain diseases. Take migraines, for example: we know there are many triggers for migraines, including bright lights, stress, dehydration and nutrient deficiencies. But in some people specific foods, such as chocolate, wine and cheese, can trigger a migraine.

'In my clinical setting, I have seen people with severe joint pains improve in weeks through cutting out specific foods from their diet. Also, with autistic children, I have been amazed at the power of food to calm aggressive behaviour, increase concentration, and even improve communication and connection.

However, I would say that food is not a replacement for medication; food can affect both the types of medication and the levels of medication needed. So if you are on medication, working with your doctor alongside a nutritionist

Diet

is recommended.'

Angelette's example of using dietary advice as a form of therapeutic intervention is borne out in emerging research.

A report by the BBC on Wednesday, 28 October, 2009, highlighted the outcome of research on curcumin, a bioactive compound found in turmeric. The research was undertaken by Dr Sharon McKenna and her team at the Cork Cancer Research Centre. They found that curcumin started to kill cancer cells within 24 hours, and that these cells began digesting themselves, after the curcumin 'triggered lethal cell death signals'.

Dr McKenna reported that: 'Scientists have known for a long time that natural compounds have the potential to treat faulty cells that have become cancerous and we suspected that curcumin might have therapeutic value.' She further stated that: 'These exciting results suggest that scientists could develop curcumin as a potential anti-cancer drug to treat oesophageal cancer.'

Responding to these findings, Dr Lesley Walker, director of cancer information at Cancer Research UK, said: 'This is interesting research which opens up the possibility that natural chemicals found in turmeric could be developed into new treatments for oesophageal cancer.' (BBC News Channel, 28 October 2009, 'Curry Spice Kills Cancer Cells'.)

Healing foods

Commencing 1 November 2011, viewers across the UK tuned into Channel 4 to watch a pioneering eight-part series

Golden Tips for those Golden Years

which examined the science behind the use of food as medicine. Entitled *The Food Hospital*, the series invited individuals suffering from a range of medical conditions and symptoms to undertake specific food treatment programmes to ascertain whether their health challenges could be alleviated by eating certain foods for a period of up to 6 weeks. Each individual received detailed consultation from three practitioners – a GP, a consultant specialising in their condition and a leading NHS dietician – indicating which foods to integrate and which foods to avoid.

The programme received mixed reviews, but what was evident in most cases was that the 'patients' attending the Food Hospital experienced a marked change in their conditions.

In addition to this, viewers were invited to take part in the first-of-its-kind television-led food science trials. Each week those participants with a particular health challenge were divided into two groups. Then each group was subjected to a specific food trial to see which food best alleviated the symptoms. As a result of the series, extended research is being undertaken with more study subjects to gather data

Diet

to establish evidence-based conclusions.

Among the foods highlighted for their therapeutic properties during these Food Hospital trials were the following:

Antioxidants – blueberries, gogi berries, kiwi fruit, pomegranates, tomatoes
Anti-inflammatory agents – cherries, flaxseed, ginger (use with caution if on blood-thinning medication), millet, turmeric
Anti-microbial agents – cranberries, broccoli, garlic (use with caution if on blood-thinning medication), pomegranates
Blood sugar balancers – barley, chickpeas, cinnamon, lentils, oats, soya beans, sweet potatoes
Brain boosters – avocados, bananas, oats, walnuts
Cardiovascular health aids – almonds, avocados, celery, garlic, oats
Digestive aids – cabbages, fennel, ginger, pineapple
Detoxifying agents – beetroot, fennel, prunes
Immunity boosters – asparagus, garlic, kiwi fruit,

Golden Tips for those Golden Years

spinach, watercress
Skin health aids – carrots, cucumbers, millet, turmeric.

The British Dietetic Association has produced some factsheets on well-researched studies relating to diet and health. The reports identify specific health conditions, and suggest foods which may work best for those conditions and the dietary practices that can enhance well-being. Visit *www.bda.uk.com/foodfacts* for more details.

Excellent books on nutrition by Professor Winston Craig include *Nutrition & Wellness*, second edition (2011); *Flavonoids, Food and Your Future* (2009); and *Herbs for Your Health – A Guide to the Therapeutic Use of 45 Commonly Used Herbs*, second edition (2011). In addition to these sources, try Dr Clemency Mitchell's book, *Understanding Nutrition*, which is available from the Stanborough Press.

Water

Water

Adequate hydration is crucial to life and the optimum cell function of all our body systems. Known as the 'elixir of life', water has for centuries been hailed for its therapeutic properties.

When advocating the beneficial use of water, E. G. White wrote: *'In health and in sickness, pure water is one of heaven's choicest blessings. Its proper use promotes health. It is the beverage which God provided to quench the thirst of animals and man. Drunk freely, it helps to supply the necessities of the system and assists nature to resist disease.' The Ministry of Healing*, p. 237.

Golden Tips for those Golden Years

Water benefits

In his book *Hydro-Hygiene: The Science of Curing By Water*, Dr R. Lincoln Graham, MD, promotes the beneficial elements of water. Commenting on the general trend to underestimate its value, he states: 'If the medical profession is ever called upon to answer in a high court for its sins of omission, one of the first questions it will have to meet will be, "Why have you, for almost twenty centuries, neglected to use water as a therapeutic agent?" '

Due to her interest in health, Millie Williams, Health Ministries leader, decided to put a 'water challenge' to the members of Chiswick Seventh-day Adventist Church. The task: to cut out all fizzy and box drinks and replace those beverages with water for one month. Participants were to have no less than eight 8oz glasses of water per day, or the equivalent of 1.5 litres. The option of some freshly squeezed fruit juices (for those who found the sole use of water difficult) was allowed.

At the end of four weeks an evaluation was undertaken to ascertain the impact of the water challenge. The results were remarkable. Among the participants, the following outcomes were reported:

- Concentration improved.
- Constipation was replaced with freer bowel movements.
- Headaches were alleviated.
- Lower back pain disappeared.
- Skin problems cleared (blemishes which had previously not improved with medicated creams).

Water

- Sleep was enhanced – both quality and quantity.
- Weight was lost (where previously individuals had been unable to shift excess weight).

Individually, our requirements for water may differ according to our age, gender, body weight, temperature, dietary practice and intensity of exercise.

Water – how much is enough?

An adult's total body weight is composed of 55-70% water. All our body systems depend on water. For instance, water carries nutrients to our cells, flushes toxins out of vital organs, and provides a moist environment for tissues such as those in the ear, nose and throat.

We lose water daily through breathing, perspiration and the excretion of urine and faecal matter. Key to optimal functioning of the body, its water supply needs to be replenished through the consumption of fluids and foods.

We acquire water from three sources: fluids (plain water and other beverages), foods (particularly fruits and vegetables) and as a by-product of chemical reactions in the body.

There are varying recommendations as to how much water is enough. A BBC News online article dated 2 April 2008 compared recommendations from the Food Standards Agency and the British Nutrition Foundation, which revealed the following:

Golden Tips for those Golden Years

- In the UK, the Food Standards Agency's 'Eatwell' website recommends that we drink six to eight small glasses of fluid a day – equivalent to 1.2 litres. This was, however, based on studies of fluid lost daily by the body, rather than suggested 'health benefits'.
- The British Nutrition Foundation, however, suggests slightly more and advises individuals to take between 1.5 and 2 litres daily.

Most people have heard other advice, such as drinking eight 8-ounce glasses of water daily (around 1.9 litres). The Mayo Clinic states: 'Although the "8 by 8" rule isn't supported by hard evidence, it remains popular because it's easy to remember. Just keep in mind that the rule should be reframed as: "Drink at least eight 8-ounce glasses of fluid a day", because all fluids count toward the daily total.'

Other observations from the Institute of Medicine recommend higher amounts:

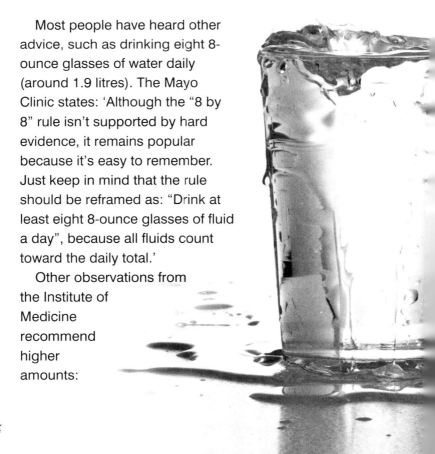

Water

'The Institute of Medicine recommends that men consume 3 litres (about 13 cups) of total beverages a day and women consume 2.2 litres (about 9 cups) of total beverages a day. These guidelines are based on national food surveys that assessed people's average fluid intakes.' *About.com*, 'Sports Medicine' (6 February, 2008).

Factors influencing water requirements

As already mentioned, several factors influence our requirement for water, including age, gender, body weight, temperature, dietary practice and exercise intensity. The Mayo Clinic reports that we may need to adjust our water intake depending on our health status and level of activity, the climate and whether we're pregnant or breastfeeding (*www.mayoclinic.com/health/water/NU00283*).

Here are their recommendations:

Exercise

- If engaging in activity that makes you sweat, you need to compensate for the fluid loss by drinking extra water.
- Take 400-600 millilitres (approximately 1.5 to 2.5 cups) during short bouts of exercise. However, intense exercise of more than an hour requires a higher fluid intake.

Golden Tips for those Golden Years

Environment
- When the weather is hot or humid it can make you sweat more, and this requires that you increase your fluid intake.
- You can also lose moisture from your skin during wintertime due to heated indoor air.
- When at altitudes of 8,200 feet (2,500 metres) or greater you may experience more rapid breathing and increased urination, both of which will use up more of your fluid reserves.

Illnesses and health conditions
- Your body loses additional fluids during a fever, diarrhoea or vomiting. Drinking more water is advised at this time. Your doctor may also recommend oral remedies to rehydrate you in some cases.
- With some conditions, such as bladder infections or urinary tract stones, practitioners will advise an increased fluid intake.
- In other cases, however, health conditions like heart failure and some types of kidney, adrenal or liver disease can restrict water excretion to the extent that fluid intake must also be reduced.

Pregnancy and breastfeeding
- Expectant mothers or those breastfeeding need more fluid to maintain hydration.
- The Mayo Clinic Institute of Medicine's recommendation for pregnant women is 2.3 litres

Water

(about 10 cups of fluids) daily, and for breastfeeding women it increases to 3.1 litres (around 13 cups) daily.

Getting the balance right

It is important to achieve a good balance when ingesting water. Too much can lead to water intoxication and too little can cause dehydration. Here is what can happen:

Water intoxication occurs when excessive water is ingested (usually very quickly). This dilutes the blood content, leading to a condition called hyponatraemia, where blood salt levels become dangerously low, affecting brain, heart and muscle function.
- Symptoms include dizziness, nausea, headaches and disorientation. Swelling of the brain and lungs can also occur, leading to death.

Dehydration occurs when there is insufficient water in the body to carry out normal function. Symptoms include:
- Mild cases – dark urine, dry skin and mouth, lethargy.
- Severe cases – muscle spasms, racing pulse and seizures.
- Dehydration in seniors has often led to poor brain health, increased infection risk and frailty, all of which increase the risk of premature death.

Correct levels of hydration will produce clear or straw-coloured urine.

Golden Tips for those Golden Years

Water – therapeutic external use

'There are many ways in which water can be applied to relieve pain and check disease. All should become intelligent in its use in simple home treatments. Mothers, especially, should know how to care for their families in both health and sickness.' Ministry of Healing, p. 237.

The term 'hydrotherapy' refers to the therapeutic use of water in the treatment of certain health conditions. The Bluebell Physiotherapy and Hydrotherapy Practice states: 'In terms of improvements to blood and lymph circulation, the relaxing of tension in the tissues, the alleviation of pain and the calming of the nervous system, hydrotherapy is at least as effective, and often more effective, than drug treatments.'
(www.bluebellspa.co.uk/techniques/hydrotherapy)

The Bluebell Practice identifies the following hydrotherapy benefits:

- Dramatically increased elimination of waste, which assists detoxification.
- Loosening of tense, tight muscles, which encourages relaxation.
- Increased metabolic rate and digestion activity.
- Cell hydration, which improves skin and muscle tone.
- Boosting of the immune system, allowing for more efficient function.
- Improved function of internal organs by stimulating their blood supply.

Hydrotherapy works by using water as a vehicle for

Water

transporting heat and cold. The application of warm or hot water causes arteries and veins to expand, bringing additional blood and lymph fluid to a specific area. The application of cold water causes the constriction of arteries and veins, thereby forcing blood and lymph outward. This movement of blood and lymph encourages oxygenation, nutrient absorption and the removal of toxins and waste products.

The use of hydrotherapy involves varied techniques. These include the use of water in any of its three states – solid (ice); liquid; and gaseous (steam). Among the treatments are hot and cold showers, hot and cold baths for limbs, fomentation (hot and cold compresses), water-soaked towels and sheets, sponge baths for fever, and hot foot baths.

Golden Tips for those Golden Years

Some hydrotherapy cautions, contra-indications and risks (www.thebodyworker.com)

- Hydrotherapy is contraindicated in patients with skin conditions.
- Diabetics should avoid full-body wraps and hot applications to their feet or legs.
- Sufferers of Raynaud's disease should avoid cold applications.
- If pregnant or suffering from abnormally high or low blood pressure, heart disease, diabetes, multiple sclerosis or peripheral vascular disease, hot immersion baths and long, hot saunas are not recommended.
- If suffering from rheumatism, sciatica, pelvic inflammation or bladder or rectal irritation, cold foot baths are not recommended.
- The elderly and young children should avoid full-body hot treatments as they could become exhausted due to the excess heat.

Trust in God

Faith and healing

'The Saviour would have us encourage the sick, the hopeless, the afflicted, to take hold upon His strength. Through faith and prayer the sickroom may be transformed into a Bethel [house of God] . . . and this conviction will itself do much for the healing of both the soul and the body.' *Ministry of Healing*, ch. 16, p. 226.

While several studies have reported the beneficial health outcomes of individuals practising their faith, the most convincing evidence-based reports to date have been about emotional well-being. The Mental Health Foundation (2007) study titled 'Keeping the Faith – Spirituality and Recovery From Mental Health Problems' identified that certain aspects of religious and spiritual involvement are associated with positive mental health outcomes.

Just a couple of years earlier, the Royal College of Psychiatrists' research (*Spirituality and Mental Health*, 2005) discovered that mental health service users highlighted the importance of their faith in God as a key aspect to their recovery. As a result these service users reported better depression recovery, improved self-control, raised self-esteem, increased confidence and better relationships.

Another study published by the Mental Health

Golden Tips for those Golden Years

Foundation (2006) identified that people with severe mental health problems, across a range of diagnosed conditions, found significant benefits to having a faith which they practised. The results revealed that 60 per cent of these individuals reported that their religious experience or spirituality was very helpful, and had 'a great deal' of beneficial impact on their illness. This was particularly related to the feelings that religion and spirituality fostered, and the positive emotions of being 'cared for' and not being alone. *Mental Health, Religion and Culture* (2004).

In a BBC 2 *Horizon* documentary aired on Tuesday 19 February 2008, a correlation was made between the strong religious beliefs of those who practised their faith, and the positive response to stress that they demonstrated. Researcher Dr Kelly Morton, who was interviewed in the documentary, made this point: 'There are many stressors in life that we cannot control. . . . Connection to something higher than oneself, connection to the sacred, connection to a tight-knit religious community allows you to modulate your reactions, your emotions, to believe that there is a broader purpose and therefore your body can stay in balance and not be destroyed by those stressors and traumas over time.'

Trust in God

The Adventist impact

The world-renowned Adventist Health Studies are long-term projects involving Seventh-day Adventists. They explore the links between Adventist lifestyle and diet, and the incidence of disease. It is not surprising, then, that the faith aspects of Adventists have captured the interest and attention of scientists for several years.

Currently, more than 96,000 church members from the US and Canada are participating in the Adventist Health Study-2, conducted by researchers at the Loma Linda University School of Public Health. In previous research on Adventists, lower levels of stress were linked to their strong faith in God, active religious lifestyle and close community spirit (*www.adventisthealthcare.com*).

However, in a recent study entitled *Adventist Religion and Health Study* (2006 – present) the spiritual impact of the Adventist faith on health is being examined in more detail.

Golden Tips for those Golden Years

Here are some preliminary findings from the current study (*http://www.llu.edu/public-health/health/adventist-religion-health.page*):

- The advantage Adventists have over non-Adventists for mental health is greater in older age groups than in younger ones.
- Participants who engaged in secular activities on Sabbath had poorer reported physical health.
- Those who said Sabbath relieved tensions and promoted feelings of calm and peace reported better mental health.
- Religious individuals had fewer negative emotions.
- Those who experienced an abusive home environment had more negative emotions. These negative emotions predict worse physical health.
- Divorced persons had more depressive symptoms than the non-divorced, but divorced individuals who used positive religious coping mechanisms had fewer depressive symptoms than those who did not use positive religious coping mechanisms. The three types of positive religious coping mechanisms that were inversely associated with depressive symptoms were:
  - *Collaborative religious coping:* Defined as forming a problem-solving relationship with God. Respondents identified a caring and powerful God, active in individual lives.
  - *Benevolent religious reappraisals:* Problems are reinterpreted as part of a divine plan or as an opportunity for growth.

Trust in God

- *Seeking spiritual comfort from God:* Defined as engaging God through prayer or other devotional practices.

Other research findings from non-religious healthcare providers are now acknowledging the relationship between spirituality and positive health outcomes.

In a study on spirituality and health, Harvard professor Anne Harrington argues that spirituality is important to health because of the following:[1]

- It promotes a healthy lifestyle and provides good community.
- Contemplative practices reduce stress.
- Belief is a healing power.

---

[1] *Harrington, A. (2004), 'The Four Arguments',* Spirituality and Health, *February 2004, pp. 46-51.*

Golden Tips for those Golden Years

Maintaining health during illness

As we conclude this little volume on golden health tips for longevity we examine the importance of pursuing a healthy lifestyle during recovery from illness.

My story:

Following a head injury in October 2011 I was diagnosed with protracted post-concussion syndrome and advised to rest and spend no more than 10 minutes at a time at the computer, watching TV, or reading – and especially to avoid small print.

However, when my concussion symptoms persisted, I decided to review the 'Golden Eight', 'natural remedies' referred to in *The Ministry of Healing*, and upon which this book is based. I soon realised that due to the extent of the injury, several areas of my health had been compromised: I was not getting the exercise I was used to; had less exposure to sunlight and natural air; and was experiencing altered sleep, diet and mood patterns.

The impact of my enforced sedentary lifestyle became particularly evident when I ventured out with a family member one Sunday, just for a short trip to one of the local

Golden Tips for those Golden Years

shops. My consultant neurologist had advised me to commence some outdoor exercise, so I tried on an item of clothing which I thought would be suitable. When, to my surprise, I didn't fit into the garment I checked the size on the label and concluded that the manufacturer had made a mistake. I then tried on another identical garment and, when that didn't fit either, I tried to convince myself that the designer had got the size wrong. Eventually, I reluctantly purchased the next size up, realising that 6 months of inactivity had added extra adipose tissue.

Returning home I logged on to the Blue Zone Vitality Coach programme (which mirrors the Golden Eight principles), designed to get individuals fitter within 6 weeks (*www.bluezones.com*). It assesses your current health status and subsequent projected longevity; provides a corrective programme; and calibrates daily progress. Having diligently adhered to the programme and implemented the 'Golden Eight', I'm regaining the lost ground. The sunshine and fresh air boosted my mood and sleep; the exercise enhanced my levels of alertness, reduced the drowsy episodes and got rid of that extra fat! And yes, I am back to my regular-sized garments! Thank God for nature's best remedies!

A final word

A final word

The quest for long life has been humanity's pursuit since time began. We live in a world where society is chasing after the 'ideal this' and the 'ideal that'. In the process of striving for this better life, many people buy into the anti-ageing hype and those promises of quick fixes, instead of trying to improve their lifestyles. A better quality of life comes from having a daily routine which encourages good lifestyle habits on a consistent basis. This is perhaps the best advice to enhance our chances of a long, healthy and fulfilling life. It is clear that the benefit is not just in living longer, but in living a *longer and healthier life* – enabling us to enjoy both its quality and its quantity. By doing this, we not only add years to our life, but life to our years.

It is my hope that you will embrace the 'golden tips' in this publication so that as you approach the golden years of senior life you will live it to the full. As Jonathan Swift wrote, *'May you live all the days of your life.'*[1]

---

[1] A Complete Collection of Genteel and Ingenious Conversation, *B. Motte and C. Bathurst, Fleet Street, England, 1737, dialogue II, p. 159.*

Other books by Sharon Platt-McDonald

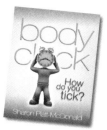

978-1-907244-14-8

978-1-907244-34-6

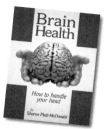

978-1-904685-88-3

978-1-907244-10-0

978-1-904685-90-6

978-1-904685-87-6

978-1-904685-86-9

978-1-904685-82-1

978-1-907244-13-1

978-1-907244-12-4

978-1-904685-81-4

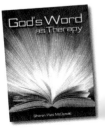

978-1-907244-11-7